Acknowledgements

Props supplied by:
Neil Street East.

First English edition published by Colour
Library Books Ltd.
© 1984 Colour Library Books Ltd.,
   Guildford, Surrey, England.
This edition published by Arlington House.
Distributed by Crown Publishers, Inc.
h g f e d c b a
Color separations by Llovet, S.A., Barcelona,
Spain.
Printed and bound in Barcelona, Spain.
by JISA-RIEUSSET and EUROBINDER.
ISBN 0 517 554852
ARLINGTON HOUSE 1984

D.L.B. 7001-84

Techniques of Sensual
MASSAGE

Janet Filderman

Photography by
Peter Barry

Designed by
Philip Clucas MSIAD

Produced by
**Ted Smart and
David Gibbon**

ARLINGTON HOUSE

Introduction

For the past twenty-five years I have been massaging and looking after the care and well-being of many clients, both famous and unknown. Yet they all have one thing in common – an appreciation of the benefits of massage and a desire to keep their bodies in good shape and healthily mobile. Massage promotes a feeling of well-being and the use of oils and creams was introduced to beautify, soften and give a therapeutic effect to the skin and muscles. Gone are the days when people thought of massage as an indulgence. Scientists now realise the potential of massage. In the next few chapters I will try to share this knowledge with you.

Although this book is intended to enable you to help yourself, why not try a professional massage at a reliable salon and experience for yourself the relaxation and toning effects that can be achieved by just one session.

The art of massage has been practised by many cultures over the centuries and it is fascinating to read of the many uses it served. For example, mention was made of athletes being massaged before the Olympic Games in 776 B.C. It is also interesting to discover the way massage grew in prestige in the ancient world and declined in esteem in the Middle Ages only to revive again in the twentieth century. In fact, when one reads the history of massage it serves as a window through which one can see the types of society at any given period. For instance, at the height of any religious fervour, massage was regarded as decadent; in societies that had a more liberal and enlightened attitude it was accepted, and its benefits recognised.

Researching into the history of massage is like discovering a see-saw of emotion because this seems to be an emotive subject surrounded by mystery – some societies welcomed the art, others were afraid of it and treated massage as evil.

The word 'massage' was not used until the 19th century when it appeared in a French/German dictionary of 1812. Before that the Greek word *tripsis* or the Latin word *frictio*, or the national equivalent, was used by writers on this subject.

In ancient documents the words 'rubbing', 'squeezing', 'pressing' or 'the laying on of hands' were recorded and friction and exercise were always linked.

An English text book written in 1866 was entitled *The Anatriptic Art*. Whilst these words continued in use until the turn of the century, the new French terms were gaining acceptance in many countries in the Western hemisphere. The French also named the different movements in massage, adding to the ancient word of 'friction'. These are now commonly known as 'effleurage', 'petrissage', 'tapotement' and 'vibrations'. Ask anyone in the street who first introduced massage and you are likely to receive the reply: "The French". But although they have developed it to a fine art, massage was around long before the French discovered it.

Chapter 1

What is Massage?

Massage, correctly given, offers relief from muscle strain. This is because when a muscle is massaged, blood is expelled from the area and when pressure is removed, fresh, newly oxygenated blood flows into the muscle, thus improving its tone. Tension is lessened by slow, rhythmic stroking, allowing the recipient to relax. The lymphatic drainage is encouraged to become more efficient and thus the clearance of toxins from the tissues and the relief of oedema is encouraged.

Friction and pressure improves circulation to the viscera and the skin develops a more glowing and healthy appearance.

All these results of massage ensure a more flexible and invigorated body, allowing the recipient to lead a fuller and more active life.

Massage is therapeutic; it can be tantalising, sensitive or sensuous – it is all up to you. You can make it fun, for it should be enjoyed.

Contra-Indications for Massage

Just as with many other forms of treatment, massage must not be given to people suffering from certain conditions or disorders. These are listed below:

Contagious or infectious
skin conditions.
Thrombosis.
Phlebitis.
Angina pectoris.
Hypertension.
Varicose veins.

Any unidentified lump or swelling. In pregnancy, the abdomen should not be massaged.

Chapter 2
The History of Massage

Since the recording of civilisation, massage has been practised by many societies.

It has taken many forms. In Babylonian and Assyrian cultures massage was used with drugs, hot and cold poultices and douches. These were supposed to act not on the patient but on the demon possessing him. It was supposed to help force out the spirit that had invaded the body and thus restore the patient to good health.

Archaeologists working in Asia Minor have found oils and perfume phials dating back to early civilisations which had been used in ritual demonstrations. Usually, they applied a solid form of perfume and oil to their heads and allowed the heat from the sun to melt the waxes, which then covered their hair and bodies before massage was given.

In ancient Egypt, the Pharaohs were annointed and massaged as a symbol of their royalty, and even in death they were massaged with embalming oils for their journey into the 'other world'. The tombs of the Pharaohs have been known to contain phials and even large jars of sweet-smelling oils for use by the Pharaoh's spirit. At that time, the lower classes were not allowed such treatments.

It is thought that the Chinese were giving massages 2,700 years before the birth of Christ. Mention of the art was recorded in one of the oldest medical works: *The Yellow Emperor's Classic of Internal Medicine*.

Taoism, attributed to Lao-Tze (604 – 541 B.C.), is a philosophy based on the idea of the natural way of harmony with nature, tranquillity and enlightenment and the Taoists practised massage and alchemy. It is

thought that Taoism, which first introduced massage to China, was at some time incorporated with kung fu.

During the Tang Dynasty (A.D. 619 – 907) four kinds of medical practitioners were recognised: physicians, acupuncturists, masseurs and exorcists. Massage at this time was highly esteemed and there was even a professor of massage working with a team of masseurs in the Imperial Medical Bureau.

During the Sung Dynasty (A.D. 960 – 1,279), massage began its decline and became the occupation of the barbers and eventually the blind were the only people allowed to practise massage, and this procedure spread to Japan.

It is interesting that with the advent in the West of the Eastern art of acupuncture, reflexology, shiatsu and kuatsu have become 'in things' to do. These forms of treatment are branches of massage which deal with the reflexes and are based on the acupuncture points in the body.

Shi means finger, *atsu* pressure. Finger pressure on the acupuncture points of the body releases the natural energies. The Japanese word *kuatsu* is a contraction of two words meaning 'life' and 'procedure' and is a Japanese technique of resuscitation mainly practised in judo, the technique resembling a pounding with fists. In Japan, it is considered a courtesy to invite visitors to take a communal bath followed by a relaxing massage. Since 600 B.C. when Hinduism first evolved out of the Verdic religion, Hindu brides have been massaged with herbs and oils prior to their wedding, to ward off evil spirits. Massage is mentioned (under the Sanskrit name of *mardan*) in the

sacred Hindu writing of the *Atharvaveda* under its medical section, the *Ayurveda*. It states that the Hindu system of medicine includes the massaging and shampooing of the skin. Reference is also given to an instrument made out of ebony and shaped like a long, thin, flat bat which was used to polish and smooth the body.

Buddhism was founded in 500 B.C. and is also associated with massage in its religious ritual. There is a relief on the Borobudur Temple, built about A.D. 800, which shows Buddha being massaged by a masseuse.

The contributions the ancient Greeks made to civilisation are numerous. One of the founders of modern massage techniques was a Greek physician who was a follower of Hippocrates, teachings; his name was Galen (A.D. 129 – 199). He resided in Rome and became physician to Marcus Aurelius. He wrote at least sixteen books related to exercise and massage. Galen classified massage into three qualities ('firm', 'moderate' and 'gentle') and three quantities ('little', 'moderate' and 'much'). By different combinations he arrived at nine forms of massage, each of which had its own indications.

Hippocrates (460 – 377 B.C.), called the Father of Medicine, was the first to set down contraindications for massage in his book *On Articulations*.

Massage in Greece is well-recorded. In his *Odyssey*, Homer speaks of beautiful women rubbing and annointing war-worn heroes to relax and revitalise them after battle.

Both the Greeks and Romans were obsessed with the 'body beautiful' and arranged games, gymnastics and competitions in large arenas to show

off their best manhood. These superb athletes became the elite, who were given their own handmaidens to bathe and massage them so that their muscles and skin would glow with good health.

Rome was founded in 753 B.C. and by 509 B.C. it had become a republic. This was to be the beginning of the great Roman influence on the world. With their conquests came organisation. The achievements of the Romans are with us still and archaeologists are still discovering the sophisticated life-style that existed at that time. During the Roman occupation of Britain, baths and massage chambers were built in each garrison town and these were extensively used by all legionairies as a daily necessity because of the effects of marching many miles on rough surfaces from one province to another.

An amusing anecdote is told of Emperor Hadrian who saw a veteran soldier rubbing himself against a marble wall at the Roman public baths and asked him why he did so. The veteran replied that he was too poor to have a slave to massage him and this was the best substitute he could find. Whereupon the Emperor gave him two slaves and enough money to maintain them. A few days later several old men rubbed themselves against the wall in the Emperor's presence, hoping for a similar good fortune but the shrewd Hadrian, perceiving their object, ordered them to massage each other. Massage was also offered to the gladiators before their entry into the arena and specially selected handmaidens were instructed in the art.

There are many other historical records of the use of massage and in looking back on the history of the art, it is interesting to see how little the practice has changed despite the advance of science and the introduction of many mechanical aids.

The Latin countries have always enjoyed the sensuous pleasures of massage and never feel guilty or remorseful, but the colder climates seem to promote feelings of embarrassment at the naked form

and even today, in the 20th century, pockets of prejudice against, and misunderstanding of, massage still exist.

Scientists have discovered that massage can release powerful, natural pain-killers in our bodies and they are working on how this can be used to alleviate pain in patients with various terminal illnesses.

With more and more emphasis being placed on fitness and health, massage becomes less the treatment for the wealthy, the athletes and the professional dancers and more a part of a keep fit routine for all people concerned with maintaining a fit and healthy body.

Chapter 3

Making Your Own Massage Oils

If at all possible, try mixing your own body oils. This can be done by mixing a small quantity of vegetable oil, such as sunflower or sesame, with a few drops of essential oil. The mixture is usually six drops of essential oil to ten millilitres of vegetable oil. The mixing of your own massage oils can be fun and at the same time it can transform an ordinary massage into something special. Given below are just some of the variations you might like to try. You can purchase the oils from any herbalist, and the two that are listed at the end of the book will send you their price lists and in some circumstances will mail the oils to you.

Basil A refreshing, uplifting essence, recommended for those who tend to be nervous. It is very good for mental fatigue.

Cedarwood The essence is distilled from the wood of the North American red cedar tree, and possesses a very long-lasting scent. It has a harmonising nature that helps stabilise unbalanced energies.

Clary-Sage A good general tonic.

Clove A spicy, carnation scent. It dispels physical and mental fatigue.

Frankincense The original 'incense' used extensively in the ancient world.

Jasmin The most exquisite, rich, floral scent. It is a euphoric and is also a strong, sensual stimulant.

Lavender One of the most popular and useful oils. It is an antiseptic and a splendid restorative when one is mentally or physically exhausted.

Lemon Grass This comes from Indo-China and has an uplifting, sweet, lemony scent.

Linden Blossom A delightful and luxurious scent. This oil relieves tension. A good oil to massage with before sleep.

Marjoram Its herbal scent has a very strong calming effect. Good for insomnia.

Myrrh Has strong healing and rejuvenating properties.

Orange This oil contains Vitamin C. It is uplifting and refreshing.

Peppermint It has cooling properties and is good for sunburn.

Rose A beautiful oil, with good tonic and revitalising properties.

Sandalwood One of the oldest and most revered essential oils, from Mysore, India. It has a sweet and woody scent and provides a quietening, meditative effect.

Ylang-Ylang A sweet, exotic scent from the Middle East. It is revitalising and good for the sympathetic nervous system.

When mixing your oil, it is preferable to put it into the dark-brown bottles obtainable from your local chemist. It should be kept in a cool, dark place when not in use.

Chapter 4

Treatments Prior to Massage

Heat Treatment

Infra-red heat treatment is used prior to massage in order to ease strain and tension from the muscles and to enable you to massage without causing damage to an area that is already under stress.

The effects of infra-red are most soothing and beneficial and should you possess one of these machines I would certainly suggest that you carry out this treatment before you begin your massage.

In addition to relaxing the body, it soothes the nerves and also, by increasing the blood supply to the area, increases nourishment to the skin and helps in the removal of waste products.

When you use an infra-red lamp, it should be positioned 24 – 28 inches away from the body and the time allowed should be no more than 10 minutes.

Cover the eyes with dampened cotton-wool and, if contact lenses are worn, these should be removed prior to treatment.

Prolonged treatment with infra-red, particularly on the back, can cause headaches, so provided the treatment is given as recommended by the manufacturer, I would suggest that you begin your massage with this treatment and end the massage with the solarium treatment.

Ultraviolet Ray (Sun-Lamp) Treatment

There are two types of sun-lamp available for home use. One is the lamp which gives out UVB rays. These are the burning rays which can cause burning to the skin if incorrectly used. They are produced by the older type of sun-ray machine and penetrate to just below the skin

surface where they encourage the melanin level to increase, thus allowing the skin to tan. This particular ray does not usually create a tan but prepares the skin so that when you go on holiday the length of time you can actually spend in the sun is increased because your melanin factor is already activated. It also allows you to maintain a tan for longer. Usually, these machines combine infra-red and there is a separate switch to operate one or the other. The Nordic Solarium produces infra-red and ultraviolet rays, both functions being operated independently, but the latter also has a heat lamp incorporated which is not of the deep heat type and is harmless to the skin.

Timing of treatments is crucial and a maximum of 5 to 10 minutes only is needed. This should be taken as 4 minutes on the front of the body and 6 minutes on the back at a low filter and gradually built up to a maximum, with filter 5, when 15 minutes can be taken, split into 7 minutes on the front and 8 minutes on the back. This treatment is highly recommended if you are suffering from spots.

Recently, it has been found that ultraviolet treatment combined with use of the contraceptive pill can cause irregular pigmentation to occur. If you are taking medication of any type it would be advisable to consult your doctor before using any suntanning machine.

The increasingly popular sun bed, which uses UVA rays, has recently come in for some adverse publicity, mainly because of incorrect usage. These machines consist of a number of fluorescent tubes which emit medium and high UVA rays. These rays are not the burning variety, although for a decent tan one has to have a large amount of UVA rays, or a mixture of UVA and UVB rays, in order to achieve satisfactory results. It is essential in both cases to use the special dark goggles, as great damage to the eyes would result without them. Timing on the UVA machine can be longer but I would advise 30 minutes as the maximum. It is a wise precaution to take a shower before and after exposure to eliminate the possibility of skin sensitivity. Jewellery should also be removed before undertaking treatment.

Salt Rub

Another pre-massage treatment is the salt rub. This is used to help stimulate the blood flow and to eliminate the dead cells from the surface of the skin. Natural sea salt is

the best as processed salt does not have the same abrasive action.

Stand on a large bath towel on the floor and put the salt into a large basin. Take a handful of salt and, beginning at the foot, work your way from the bottom of the leg, rubbing the salt into the skin. You will find it easier if you dampen your hands as this allows the salt to stick so that you get a better friction. After you have frictioned both legs, move over the trunk of the body, continue with the arms and finally finish off with heavy friction on the back.

Shower after the friction. You will be surprised at the effect of a salt rub. Not only will your skin feel cleaner and softer but it will glow and leave you with a feeling of well-being.

Epsom Salt Bath Treatment

This is another pre-massage treatment which is used in health hydros and beauty salons. Its effect is to draw toxins, which have been trapped by a sluggish constitution, out from the tissues. The process is called osmosis and is wonderful for cellulite problems.

You need at least one hour prior to massage for this treatment. Into a fairly hot bath put three to four breakfast cups of commercial Epsom salt (this you can obtain from any chemist shop). As this is a treatment you should not wash in the bath, just rest in it, and perhaps read, or listen to your favourite radio show. You should stay in the water for at least half an hour. When the treatment is concluded, shower off the salt, wrap yourself in a large towel and go and rest on your bed for at least half an hour. You should perspire heavily and will feel rather tired. A gentle massage will guarantee a sound sleep.

Manicure and Pedicure

Manicure and pedicure are included because these can be restful treatments before a massage, and in some cases they may be the only treatments you can give in a short

period of time. The treatments take about half an hour each and, of course, you can do these treatments on yourself.

Manicure

The purpose of a manicure is to keep the nails, cuticles and hands in good condition.

A manicure will lift the nail wall and the cuticle from the nail plate and so reduce the risk of hang nails. Fragile nails can also be strengthened, and buffing promotes better circulation to the nail area and so helps to prevent nail damage.

A regular manicure treatment improves a groomed appearance and is vital for the health of the nails. It can be carried out at home with very little effort and cost.

Items Required For Manicure

Nail and cuticle clippers
Buffer   Nail-varnish remover
Paste   Cuticle oil
Emery boards   Hand Cream
Nail-brush
Orange-sticks
Cotton-wool
Tissues
Bowl of warm water

Method of Manicure

1. Remove any old polish from both hands with cotton-wool soaked in nail-varnish remover.

2. Shape nails of left hand with an emery-board; always file from the sides towards the centre. Do not file too low down on the sides of the nails as this tends to weaken them.

3. When you have completed the shaping, apply a small amount of cuticle oil to the cuticles with an orange-stick wrapped in cotton-wool. You will get the wool to adhere to the stick if you wet the stick before wrapping the cotton-wool around it. Massage the oil well into cuticles.

4. Now put the fingertips into the bowl of soapy water to soften the cuticles.

5. Shape the nails of the right hand.

6. Apply cuticle oil and massage in.

7. Dry the left hand and transfer the right hand to soak in the bowl of water.

8. Apply cuticle remover (with orange-stick) as before and around the nail, lifting the cuticle gently away from the nail-plate. Also work under the free nail edge to clean the nail.

9. Use a small nail-brush to clean the free edge of each nail and the nail-plate.

10. Dry the nails and, with a hoof stick, gently press back the cuticle. If necessary, remove any dead hang nail and torn cuticle.

11. Apply a little hand cream to the back of the hands and massage up to the wrist and over the fingers, avoiding the nail area.

12. Remove right hand from the bowl of water and carry out 8, 9, 10, and 11 as before.

13. If nail-varnish is not being worn, apply a little buffing paste and buff the nails in one direction to achieve a shine.

14. To apply nail-varnish, always use a base coat as this protects the nail from the pigment in the varnish. The first stroke should be at the centre of the nail, then a stroke across the base of the nail and now a stroke on either side of the nail.
When applying a second coat, it is done with just a single broad stroke down the centre of the nail; then move out to the edges. If using a crême polish, a top protective coat is needed but with pearlised colour no top coat is required, although several coats of the colour may be needed.

15. Use a quick-drying spray to prevent the nails from getting marked and to assist in the drying.

Pedicure

A pedicure after a tiring day can be

6. Dip the nail-brush into water and brush the cuticle and nails.

7. Dry the nails and apply a little massage cream to the foot and work up towards the ankle.

8. Treat the right foot in the same way.

9. To varnish the toenails, apply pads of cotton-wool between the toes to keep them separated. Apply a base coat followed by two applications of nail-varnish, if required.

10. Apply a protective coat.

11. Spray with fixative to help dry the nails quickly.

12. Remove toe separators.

Preparation for Massage

It is, of course, usual to have a proper massage couch, but failing this I would suggest that you put a blanket on the floor and then cover it with a large, pretty towel. Your partner should then settle down on the towel until comfortable. When you commence the massage, kneel next to your partner as this will enable you to get more pressure and will help you to give a rhythmic massage.

This method for home use is preferable to using a bed as the height and softness of a bed may cause you to strain your back.

Have towels, oil and two pillows readily available. It is important that the room should be kept warm and well-ventilated. Lighting should be kept low and noise kept to a minimum, although soft music can be played if this helps to relax your partner. Keep your partner covered, except for the area you intend massaging. This is necessary to keep the muscles warm and relaxed.

The person giving the massage should remove any rings or other jewellery, and clothes should be light and loose.

extremely beneficial and brings such relief that you feel you could go out dancing all night, when before the treatment you might not have thought this possible.

The same items are needed as for a manicure plus a large washing-up bowl and three towels.

Method of Pedicure

1. Place the feet in a bowl of warm, soapy water to which you have added a little antiseptic.

2. Take out the left foot, towel dry and remove varnish, if necessary. Use clippers to cut the nails. The nails should be cut straight across to prevent ingrowing toe-nails. If you have a hard skin scraper, use this now on the hard skin areas. To prevent infection, always remember to wipe the instruments with concentrated antiseptic.

3. Massage cuticle oil into the nails and wrap a towel around the foot. Take right foot out of the water.

4. Treat right foot as in 2 and 3. Wrap the foot in a towel and return to the left foot.

5. Apply cuticle remover and work around the cuticle, lifting it from the nail-plate with an orange-stick as for the manicure.

Chapter 5

Techniques and Movements of Massage

As this book is intended to guide you through the techniques of massage, I will use non-technical words wherever possible and limit the movements to the five basic ones listed below.

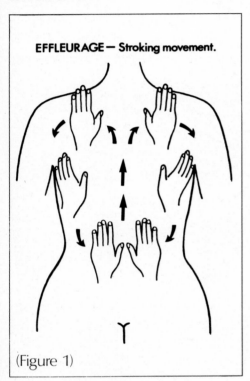

(Figure 1)

Effleurage (Figure 1)

This is the first and main movement we use and is a stroking, gliding movement. It is mainly executed with the flat of the hand and precedes all other movements. *Figure 1* will assist you in following the text.

Stroking is usually done towards the heart and the pressure should be slow and rhythmic. It should be a firm pressure on the upward stroke but light on the downward. The person being massaged should experience a continuous movement but of varied pressure.

Petrissage (Figure 2)

This is a squeezing movement, usually circular, and is applied with the thumbs and/or fingers and is mainly carried out over soft tissue that has bone immediately beneath

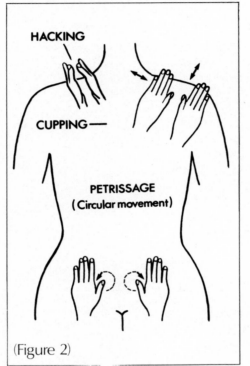

(Figure 2)

it. It helps to eliminate accumulated waste products. This movement must be performed without the sliding used in the stroking technique.

Cupping, Hacking, Pounding (Figure 2)

These movements are intended to promote circulation and improve muscle tone and are usually carried out on the back, shoulders and thigh areas.

Cupping is performed by keeping the palms arched and the fingers slightly arched but relaxed. The

fingers should be held close together. The wrist should be flexible and a tempo of 1, 2; 1, 2; should be aimed for. The sound is that of a horse trotting if the movement is carried out correctly.

Hacking is a movement which uses the sides of both hands, like a karate chop, but the fingers are kept relaxed and slightly curved. This movement is usually given on the back, shoulders, backs of the legs and buttocks. The tempo is the same as for cupping.

Pounding involves clenching the hands to form a fist and then beating lightly in the same tempo as for cupping and hacking: 1, 2; 1, 2. The effect is most beneficial over the lung area and over fatty deposits such as are found in the region of the buttocks, but the site of the kidneys should be avoided.

These are the five basic movements to a good massage. Naturally, the more sensitive and rhythmic you are, the more likely you will be able to relax and refresh your partner. Now, let us try putting some of these movements into practice.

Arm Massage (Overleaf)

Your partner adopts a semi-reclining position with their arm resting on a pillow. Kneel facing your partner and apply a small amount of oil to your hands. Now effleurage up your partner's right arm, from the back of the hand to the shoulder. Return your hands back to the starting position and repeat this movement three times.

Remember to be firm on the upstroke and lighter on the return stroke (movements **2**, **3** and **4**).

Hold the forearm with your right

2

3

4

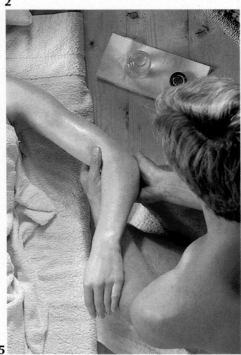

5

6

hand and with the thumb and fingers of your left hand, work up the outer part of the upper arm from the elbow to the shoulder with small circular pressures. This is the petrissage movement. Repeat this three times, always sliding down lightly to the starting position (movements **5**, **6**, **7** and **8**).

Now, repeat this movement on the inside of the upper arm by holding the forearm with the left hand and using your right thumb and fingers to massage. Repeat this three times.

7

8

Ask your partner to rest their right hand on your right shoulder and with the palms of both your hands roll up the upper arm. Start at the elbow and work up and down the arm. Do this slowly and you will feel the muscles rolling under your hands. The tempo should be 1, 2, 3 up and 1, 2, 3 down. Repeat this movement several times in a continuous, rhythmic way (movements **9** and **10**).

9

10

Gently put the arm down to your partner's side and with the knuckles of your fingers move up the side of the lower arm from wrist to elbow. Repeat three times (movements **11** and **12**).

Stroke the whole arm again from the hand to the shoulder and when you bring your hands back to the starting position, release your hands and with the thumb and first finger of both your hands hold your partner's thumb and small finger and begin small circles over the top of the fingers working to the end of the fingers and thumb. When you reach the middle finger, hold the wrist with your left hand and complete the massage of the middle finger (movements **13** and **14**).

Take hold of the little finger by the first knuckle, near the top of the finger, and give a small pull. Repeat for each finger and the thumb.

11

12

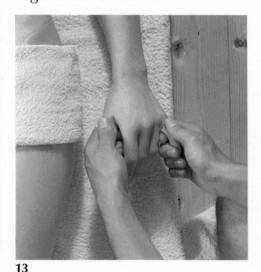

13

Turn the hand over and with your partner's palm uppermost, press the palm with the heel of your hand. This is done with circular movements. Use your left hand to support the back of the hand (movement **15**).

Finish off with the first movement – a slow stroke up the full arm. Come back to the hand with slightly increased pressure on the little finger and thumb.

15

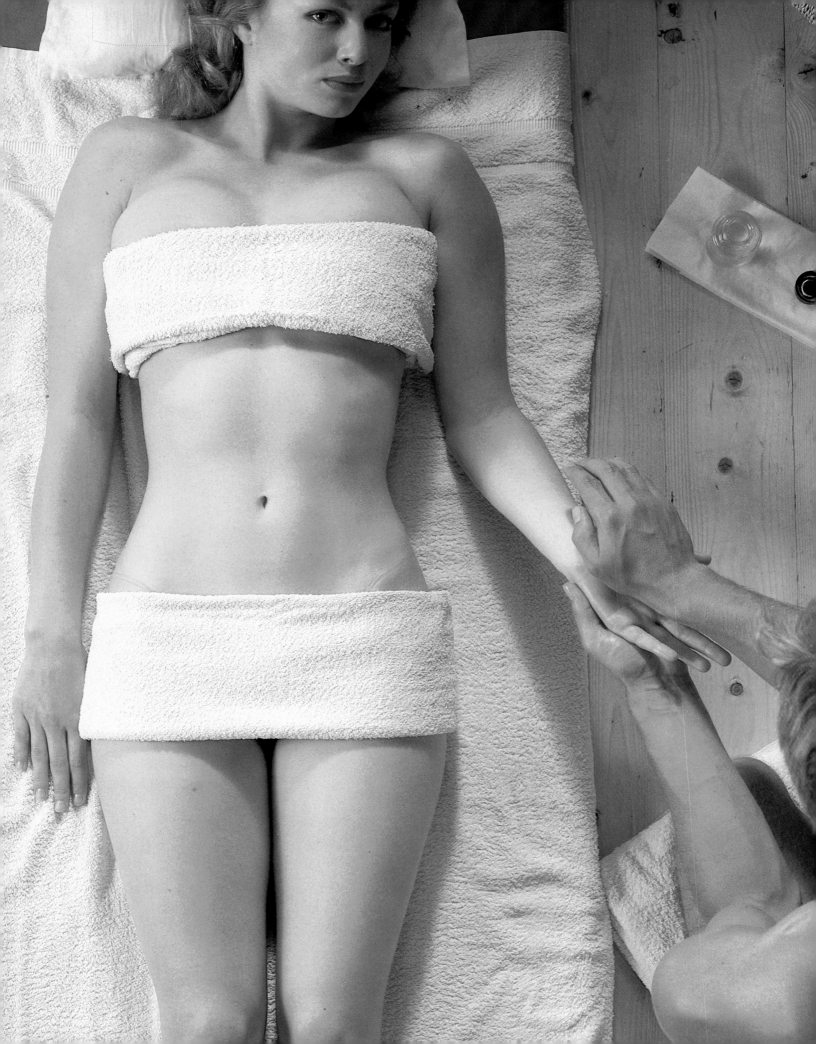

Leg and Foot Massage – Front of Right Leg

Make your partner comfortable and, if necessary, place a small pillow under their knee. Now kneel down, facing your partner.

Apply a small amount of oil to your hands and then stroke, with a broad sweep from the top of the foot, right up to the thigh and return. Your right hand should be positioned on the left side of the foot and your left hand on the right side of the foot, and when you reach the thigh your hands cross over and return down the leg back to the foot with the left hand pulling the big toe. Repeat the movement three times (movements **16**, **17**, **18**, **19** and **20**).

17

18

19

20

Now, massage the top of the foot with the full flat of the right hand. Use your left hand to hold the foot. Repeat three times.

With the thumb of both hands work up the spaces between the toes, towards the ankle. Repeat three times, slowly.

Hold the foot firmly and press it towards the ankle then rotate it one way, then the other way. Hold the heel and grasp the toes and gently pull the leg. With your hands

21

22

23

24

25

clenched, slide them up the outside of the lower leg to the knee, and return with a stroking movement with the hands open. Repeat three times (movements **21**, **22** and **23**).

Bend your partner's knee, remove the pillow and with the fingers of both hands rhythmically 'hit' the calf muscle starting from just above the ankle up to the back of the knee. Repeat three times (movements **24** and **25**.)

Place the leg back in the resting position and with both hands above the knee smooth round and under the knee. Repeat three times.

With the flat of both hands on the top of the thigh just above the knee, slide up the thigh and when you reach the groin press lightly and return your hands back to the starting position. Repeat three times (movement **26**).

With the knuckles of both hands, stroke up the inner and outer thigh

and return to the knee with the hands open. Repeat three times (movement **27**).

Now, change your position and kneel to the side of your partner, facing sideways, and begin hacking *figure 2* up to the top of the thigh from just above the knee. Try to obtain an even tempo: 1, 2; 1, 2. Repeat three times (movement **28**).

Now, cup hands with the fingers closed but relaxed and bring the hands down alternately on to the top of the thigh, work up and down and incorporate the inner thigh. If correctly done, you should have the sound of a horse trotting, as I mentioned earlier. Repeat three times (movements **29** and **30**).

End the leg massage by repeating the effleurage movement right up the leg and by pulling on the big toes, gently squeezing at the last stroke.

Move to the other side of your partner and massage the left arm and leg.

26

27

Abdomen and Rib Cage

Kneel facing your partner and with a small amount of oil on your hands sweep across the midriff and under the waist then pull gently from the spine back along the pelvis to the front of the abdomen. Repeat three times (movements **31**, **32**, **33** and **34**).

With your thumbs on the right side of the lower abdomen, slowly massage up the ascending colon, then across the top of the transverse colon and down the descending colon. Repeat this movement several times and each time slowly increase the pressure. With the heel of the hand describe circles and use gentle pressure over the same area, exactly as before. Repeat three times. Finish off with the first stroking movement (movements **35**, **36**, **37**, **38** and **39**).

31

32

33

34

35

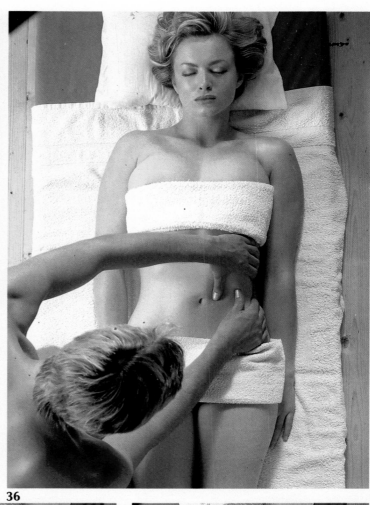

36

37

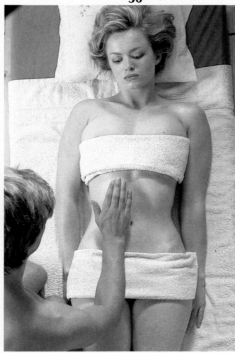

38

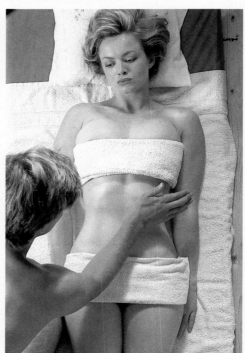

39

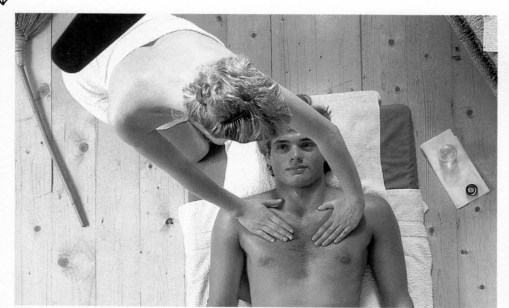

40

Now, ask your partner to turn over and we will proceed with the back.

41

42

Move up to the chest area and position yourself at your partner's head. With the fingers of both hands, circle chest wall from the centre of the sternum out towards the shoulder. When you reach the shoulders turn your hands with the palms facing you and with your fingers on the back of the shoulders. Massage along the shoulder line to the hairline, then press hard on the back of the base of the skull. Repeat several times (movements **40**, **41**, **42**, **43** and **44**).

43

Feet and Legs – Back

Put a small pillow under the ankle and, if more comfortable for your partner, under the abdomen. With a very small amount of oil on your hands, massage down the sole of the foot with the heel of your hand. Do this firmly and continuously for several movements. On the last movement, press firmly and circle each toe with the thumb of your right hand holding the foot in your left hand. Repeat the toe massage three times (movement **45**).

Move up to the heel and massage by grasping the heel with the whole hand, and your thumb pointing

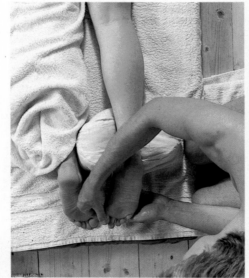

45

46

47

48

towards the toes. Finish off the foot with knuckle stroking down the sole of the foot. Use strong, firm, but slow movements to prevent tickling (movements **46, 47** and **48**).

With the palms of both hands just by the ankle in a similar position to the thigh massage earlier, slide your hands right up the whole leg from ankle to thigh and return to the ankle. Repeat this movement three times (movements **49, 50** and **51**).

Now, with the knuckles of both hands, move up from the ankle to the knee, on the outside of the lower leg. Repeat three times.

49

50

During this movement, always finish with the pressure into the 'space' at the back of the knee, using thumb pressure. Now, move up to the thigh and repeat the same movements as for the lower leg after you finished the

51

52

53

side knuckle movement. Repeat this to the centre of the thigh, over the hamstring muscles (movements **52**, **53**, **54** and **55**).

Move to the side of your partner and with your hands in a karate position, hack from the top of the thigh to the ankle and back. *Do not hack over the back of the knee.* You must try to keep the movement smooth so work slowly in the 1, 2 tempo and proceed up and down the whole leg several times. Finish off at the top of the thigh (movement **56).**

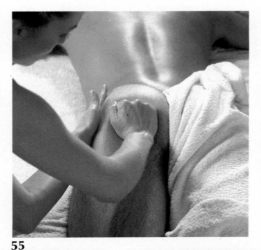

55

Make fists and pound on the top of the thigh moving slowly down to the ankle in the same manner as the hacking movement but remember not to hit the back of the knee. Finish off at the top of the thigh (movement **57**).

Finish off the leg and foot massage with three large, sweeping, stroking movements from the foot up the entire leg returning with a firm hold on the toe.

56

57

58

59

60

61

62

63

64

The Back

Position your partner with a pillow supporting the head, if necessary. The arms should be down the sides of the body allowing the shoulders to be flat and relaxed.

With your hands lightly oiled, begin at the base of the spine. Slide up to the neck and sweep your hands out across the shoulders. Move down the outside of the back to the waist and then sweep out over the hips and buttocks back to the commencement of the stroke *figure 1*. Repeat this stroking three times (movements **58**, **59**, **60**, **61**, **62** and **63**).

Move up from the base of the spine to the shoulders with the same basic movement as above. When you reach the outer shoulders make a circular movement with your fingers back to the centre of the next, then slide back to the outer shoulders and repeat this circular movement three times (*figure 2*, petrissage: movement **64**).

With your right hand on the back of the neck, squeeze slowly up the neck to the hairline. Repeat this movement and when you reach the hairline press firmly on the occipital bone with thumb and fingers (*figure 3*, back view). The movement should

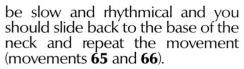

65   **66**

be slow and rhythmical and you should slide back to the base of the neck and repeat the movement (movements **65** and **66**).

Now, move out to the left shoulder and with the karate movement hack along the shoulder line. Do this three times on the left side then, without breaking the movement, continue over on the right shoulder line (movement **67**).

With the fingers of the right hand on the left shoulder by the neck and your left hand resting on top of your right hand (this gives you controlled pressure) make circular movements out towards the arm. Move your fingers down the outside of the shoulder blade coming in towards the spine and back up to the start position. Follow the contour of the shoulder and make your petrissage movements firm and rhythmic. Never try to rush massage movements. Repeat this massage three times, ending up by the neck, and then work out over the right shoulder in exactly the same manner. Finish the movement at the centre of the neck (movements **68**, **69** and **70**).

67

Now form your hands into fists and start to pound across the shoulders, down each side of the spine to the buttocks using more pressure for the

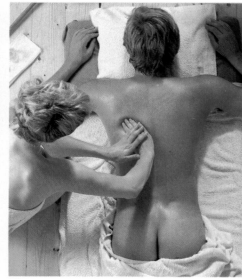

68   **69**   **70**

71

72

73

buttock area. Continue up and down for several movements and finish off at the buttocks (movements **71**, **72** and **73**).

Form hands into the cupping position and work up and over the buttocks and back with vigorous and rhythmic cupping movements. Repeat at least three times (movements **74**, **75**, and **76**).

By now, your partner's skin should have a pink glow. Finish off at the buttocks and then, with the knuckles of your right index and middle fingers, slide up each side of the spine to the top of the neck (movements **77** and **78**).

With both hands, press firmly down the back, close to each side of the spine. Your fingers should be pointing outwards and you should work down towards the buttocks (movements **79** and **80**).

Finish off with the effleurage movement, three times.

Now, fully cover your partner and allow them to relax. Remember to keep your partner covered during the massage except for the part on which you are working.

74

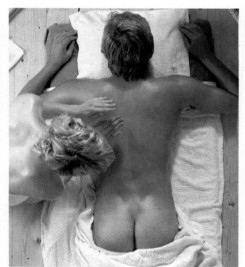

75

76

77

78

79

80

Electric Hand Massagers

These machines are designed for home use and are intended to take the hard work out of massage, but nothing can replace a good hand massage. However, for larger muscle areas such as the thighs, buttocks and back a massager can help.

Many salons combine both hand massage with a gyrating massage machine, to achieve both a stimulating and relaxing condition. When using these machines, the following rules must be observed. Because of the heat generated by the electric massager, talcum powder must be used on the body at the commencement of the massage and the machine should only be used for a maximum of ten minutes and then rested and allowed to cool down. There are various heads supplied with the machine and you will get better results if you take the trouble to change the heads when dealing with different areas of the body that call for varying degrees of pressure. As you follow the sequences photographed in this book, you will observe the constant change of heads used throughout the movements.

82

Arm Massage

Begin by stroking the talc up the arm. Hold the arm underneath the forearm with the left hand; keep your thumb low and with the right hand holding the massager, gently place it on the forearm just above the wrist and circle up the arm. When you reach the upper arm move your left hand further up to support the upper arm (movements **81**, **82**, **83** and **84**).

Do not come down the arm with the massager, just lightly glide back to the start position and begin the sequence again.

The upper arm should be massaged first on the inside, then from the centre up to the top of the arm, finishing on the outer plane of the arm from the elbow upwards. Massage rhythmically and always up towards the heart.

83

84

Leg Massage

Remember to change the massage head to a stronger one. Talc the leg from the ankle to the top of the thigh. Ask your partner to bend their knee and now begin on the outer side of the lower leg from just above the ankle bone up to the side of the knee. Return to the ankle and repeat the movement three times. Move the massager to the inner calf and repeat the movement (movements **85** and **86**).

Straighten the leg and move up to the thigh. Begin on the outer side of the thigh, from the side of the knee up to the top of the thigh. Repeat this movement three times and then move to the inner thigh and continue as before and always in three movements to give rhythm. Finish on

85

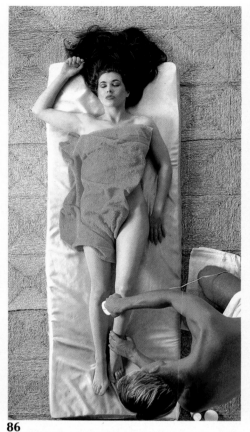

86

87

the middle of the thigh from just above the knee to the groin. Do not massage over the knee itself. Always aim to give slow, circular movements as you would in hand massage (movements **87**, **88**, **89** and **90**).

88

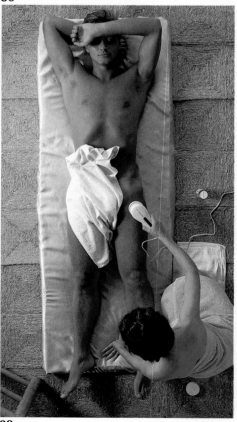

89

91

92

93

Abdomen Massage

Change the head of the massager to a soft sponge applicator and talc your partner's abdomen. Begin at the bottom right hand side and gently follow the ascending colon, work along the transverse colon and down the descending colon – in fact, follow the digestive tract. Remember to keep a steady pressure (movements **91**, **92** and **93**).

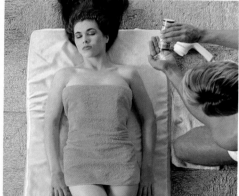

94

Chest Massage

First apply talc then, using the same applicator head as for the abdomen, move across the upper chest working in circles from the middle of the chest out to the left and back to the middle and out to the right. Go over the area three times, finishing on the right shoulder (movements **94**, **95**, **96**, **97**, **98** and **99**).

95

96

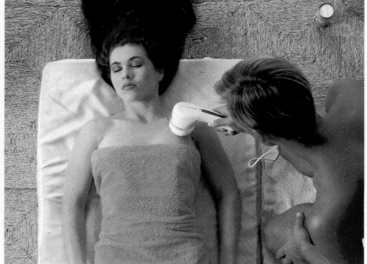

97

98

99

Leg Massage – (Back)

Change the massage head to a hard stimulator, talc the leg from the ankle to the top of the thigh. Commence just above the ankle and move over the back of the calf muscle up as far as the crease at the back of the knee. Glide the massager back to the start of the movement and repeat three times (movements **100** and **101**).

Continue up the leg to the outer thigh, then the inside thigh, finishing off on the centre of the thigh, working up the hamstring muscles to just below the buttock. All the movements should be repeated three times (movements **102**, **103**, **104**, **105** and **106**).

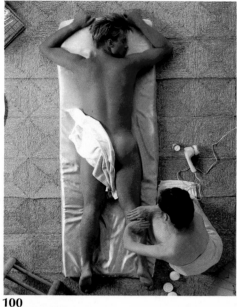

100

101

102

103

104

105

106

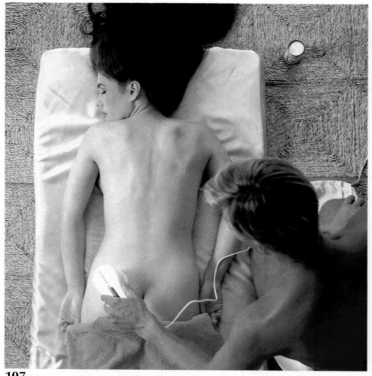

107

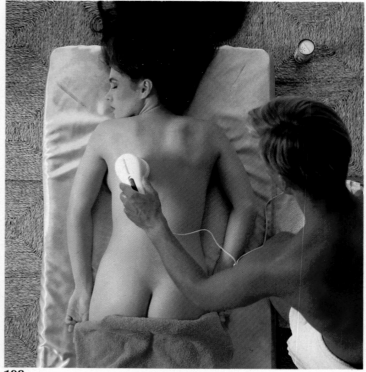

108

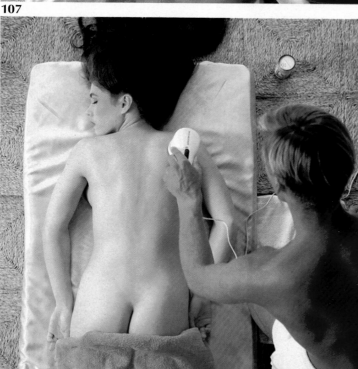

109

110

Back Massage

Talc the back and work up one side of the back from the buttock to the shoulder and repeat on the opposite side. Begin the massage with the same hard applicator head as for the back of the legs but after working the back three times with the hard head change to a soft applicator and spend a little longer working on the shoulder and neck area to ease out the stress and tension which accumulates in this area (movements **107**, **108**, **109**, **110** and **111**).

Head Massage

A special spiky applicator head is used for this type of massage. Work over the scalp in circular movements from the base of the skull up one side of the head to the hairline and begin again on the other side of the head from the base of the skull to the hairline.

The scalp is the only part of the body on which you do not use talc before commencing the massage.

When you have finished using the massager, clean the heads with warm, soapy water and dry well. Do not use dirty heads on another person as this could carry skin infections.

Chapter 6

Passive Exercise Machines

"What is meant by passive exercise?" I am repeatedly asked this question. "Does it work?" is another. In this section, I hope to answer not only these two fundamental questions but to clear up some wrong impressions which have been formed about this type of exercise. Passive exercise is a form of treatment which shortens muscle. When you perform ordinary, physical exercise, your muscles are caused to contract by electrical impulses transmitted from your brain. Passive exercise machines reproduce these impulses through electric pads placed on the muscles, making them contract at a controllable rate.

Machines of this type can allow you to lose inches and will, therefore, certainly alter body shape. It is an ideal home treatment and if you happen to be a very busy person who cannot afford at least forty minutes a day to do physical exercise, then this is the answer for you because you need only use these machines regularly for fifteen to thirty minutes to achieve results and at the same time you can read, watch television, do some paperwork or telephone friends – what could be easier?

One of the reasons these machines are not as popular as they should be is the fact that when they were first introduced on to the market they were said to be 'slimming machines', and the general public immediately thought this meant that they would be able to lose weight without having to diet or give up alcohol. This is far from the truth. The only way you can lose weight is by watching your intake of food and alcohol. One can, however, streamline and alter body shape with the aid of these machines.

112

Another factor involved is the correct pad placement on the body. If this is not done correctly, then of course the muscles will not contract and the results will not be successful.

I feel it is important for anyone buying these faradic machines to have correct tuition on their use before they purchase one, and most reputable companies will give this tuition. The instruction booklet that accompanies the equipment should be studied, and any query should be discussed with the manufacturer before using the machine.

These machines need water on the pads to allow the conductivity of the electric current to the muscle, and I have found that many people are too unsure to wet the pads sufficiently for the impulse to operate correctly. It is preferable if you are padding up a large area to apply a little KY Jelly to the pad so that it retains the water during the treatment period and

prevents the pad from drying out. When the pads are too dry, the electric current tends to feel stingy and uncomfortable.

The duration of the treatment on this type of machine should be a maximum of half an hour on the body and no more than 15 to 20 minutes on the face and neck. The face and neck uses a special attachment to the main machine which is usually sold as an extra.

Just as you are expected to maintain a daily physical exercise programme, so, if you wish to see results with the passive exercise machine you should use it daily for half an hour, or at the very least three times a week.

There are many of these types of machine available on the market and before purchasing one I suggest you ensure that you can get instruction on its use together with a treatment, so that you can experience how it feels and works when correctly applied.

Some of the makes I can recommend are Jimbody (a French machine and the one demonstrated in this book), Slendertone, Contour and Vitatone.

The Placement of Pads and Operation (photo 112)

Make yourself comfortable. You will need to have by you a bowl of water, KY Jelly if possible (obtainable from any chemist), towels, a book, pen and paper, the telephone and anything you wish to do whilst you are exercising.

Consider which layout you wish to use and then unroll the straps and place them around the area to be treated. Study the pad placement; these will be shown in your instruction book but the more important ones are given in this book for your information.

Wet the pads thoroughly. Place a little of the KY Jelly onto the pads (black side to the skin on the Jimbody model) and now you are ready to operate the controls and set your exercise going.

Abdomen Layout for Women This is a good layout for general sagging around the abdomen and reducing waist measurements (photographs **113**, **114**, **115** and **116**).

Abdomen Layout for Men A particularly good layout for men. It strengthens the muscles which prevent the stomach from sagging (photograph **117**).

113

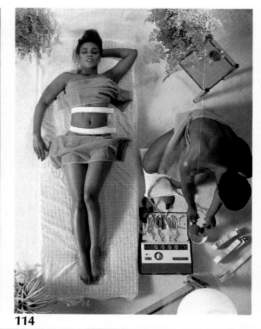

114

115

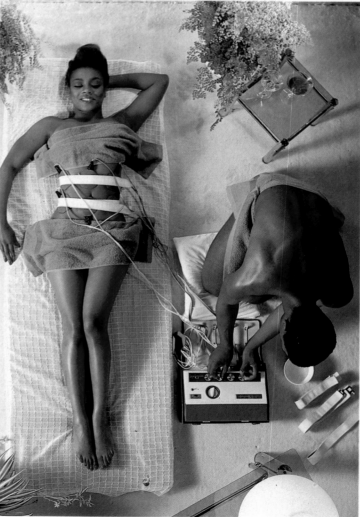

116

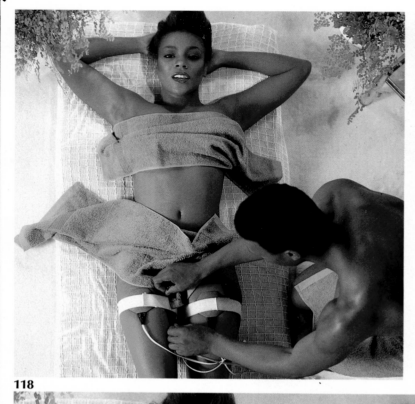

118

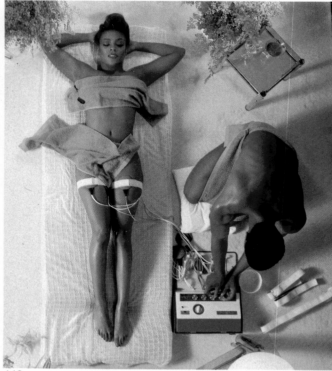

119

120

121

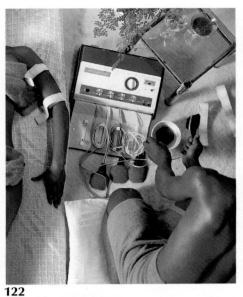

122

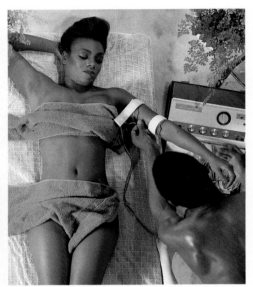

123

124

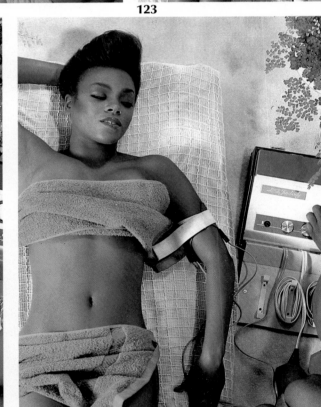

125

Front Thighs This layout gives a good treatment to very flabby tops of the thighs (photographs **118** and **119**).

Breasts This layout firms the pectoral muscles on which the breasts lie and also the wall of the chest (photograph **120**).

Toning of Flabby Underarms (photographs **121**, **122**, **123** and **124**). **Improving the Upper Arm Muscles** (photograph **125**).

126

127

129

128

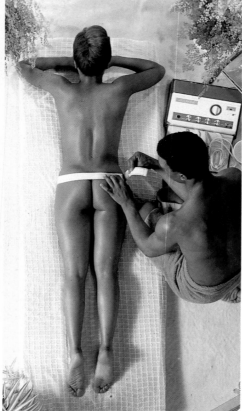

130

Back, Hips and Back of Legs This layout strengthens the back, neck and shoulder muscles and aids relaxation (photographs **126** and **127**).

For use on a flabby back and side areas (photograph **128**).
A good, general treatment for hips and the backs of legs (photographs **129**, **130** and **131**).

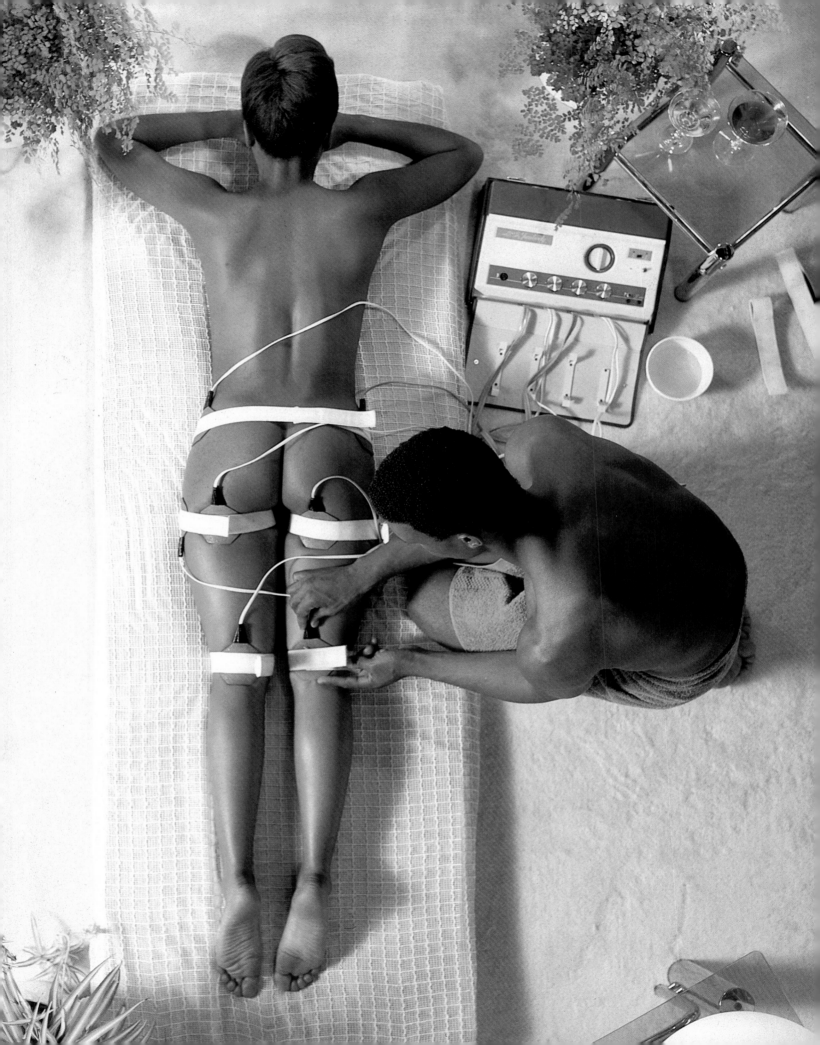

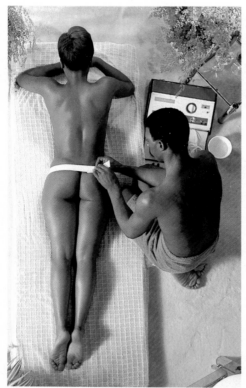

132

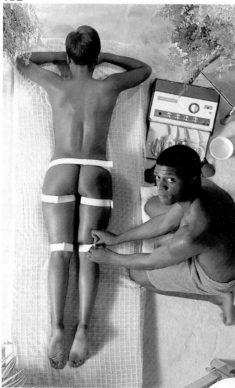

133

A layout to exercise and firm buttocks and inner thighs (photographs **132**, **133** and **134**).

135

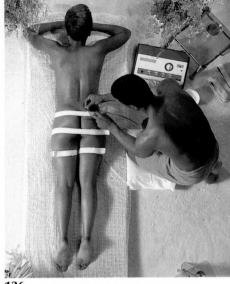

136

of prolonged disuse or incorrect use; the abdominal muscles on women being an example where overweight and poor muscle tone causes abdominal contents to press outwards against the muscular abdominal wall causing a protrusion. To firm and tone the pectoral muscles underlaying the breasts particularly after childbirth and lactation.

To maintain an attractive firm figure and prevent sag.

Contra-indications

Pregnancy.
Damaged tissue or areas of injury.
Heart disorder.
If in doubt, consult your doctor.

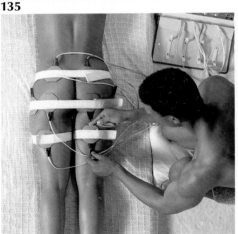

137

For general toning of buttocks and the backs of thigh muscles (photographs **135**, **136**, **137** and **138**).

Indications for the Use of the Passive Exercise Machine

Where figure re-shaping or reduction in inches is required.

For post-natal rehabilitation of the waistline.

For toning and firming the contours whilst body weight is being lost through diet.

To reshape or tone thighs or buttocks which are out of proportion to the figure or inclined to fatty deposits.

To re-educate muscle tissue which has become poor in tone as a result

Chapter 7

Facial Massage

To get the maximum benefit from a well-executed facial massage, it would be advantageous to prepare the skin beforehand.

The first principle, therefore, is to cleanse the skin with a good, gentle, proprietary brand of skin cleanser. This is because oil carries the dissolver in the cleanser into the pores and helps to unplug the debris that builds up in the skin.

Work the cleanser well into the neck and face, applying it in upward movements. Pay particular attention to the crease in the chin and the sides of the nose. It is best to use your fingers to do this because this works the cleanser in better. Remove with tissues and repeat the cleansing procedure for a second time.

If you do not have a facial sauna machine you can still carry out the next stage with a kettle of boiling water. Pour the water into a basin and allow it to fill to a depth of about three inches. Throw in a handful of herbs – either sage, peppermint, camomile flowers, marigold petals, or lavender flowers. All of these herbs have either healing properties or smell nice, or both. Cover your head with a towel and hold your face in the steam for at least ten minutes.

Towel dry the face and then, if there are any blackheads on the nose or chin, use a blackhead extractor to remove them. This is a small steel instrument like a thin pencil, with a small spoon-shaped opening. You press the hole over the blackhead and it will pop up through the hole. Never squeeze a spot or blackhead with your fingers because there are many fine blood capillaries just under the skin and if these become broken, the blood seeps into the tissue and it cannot be dispersed without medical intervention. Blackhead extractors can be purchased at any good chemist or medical supply showroom.

The next stage in preparing the face for massage is a mask treatment. There are many on the market but it is fun to make your own and it costs very little – just raid your fridge and kitchen. Two which I use often, one of which is for pre-party occasions, are made with an egg.

The first mask is a gentle one for all skin types. Separate an egg and put the yolk into a small basin, add six drops of almond oil and mix. Apply it with a pastry brush to your face and neck. Avoid the eye area and, if you can, put a thin slice of cucumber on each eye. Then rest for ten minutes. Rinse away with warm water. Towel dry.

Cucumber is wonderfully cooling and will help to take down swellings from the eyes. It is marvellous after a bad night. Another good eye pad from your kitchen is grated potato. This should be put into old handkerchiefs or gauze and placed on the eyes. Potato acts like a magnet to draw out inflammation and is very good for eyes that suffer from smoke. The second egg mask uses the egg white. Whisk up the white just to break it and then add a few drops of lemon juice. Apply to the face and neck with a brush and leave on for ten minutes. This is a slightly astringent mask and is a wonderful pre-party treatment as it leaves the skin glowing and is an excellent pick-me-up. Remove the mask with warm water and towel dry.

One final mask is for damaged or lined skins. Heat up a teaspoonful of olive oil (or avocado oil) in an egg cup in the warming drawer of your cooker. Work the warm oil into the face and neck, including the eye area and again rest for ten minutes with your eyes covered with cooling eye pads. This is the only mask that you do not have to rinse off before the facial massage.

For spotty or very greasy skin, it is a good treatment to give a few minutes, no more than five, of ultraviolet ray treatment. This must always be done with the eyes covered and the face completely free of oil.

Facial Massage

If there is time, try the pre-facial treatments first.

Make sure the face is free of make-up and the day's accumulation of grime and apply a small amount of massage cream or oil to the face and neck, working from the neck up to the forehead. Now we are ready to begin a face massage.

1. Start with the hands at the centre of the forehead. First the right hand glides from the forehead and before it reaches the hairline the left hand follows the same movement. Let the hands follow in a continuous movement and use gentle but firm pressure. Work three movements in the centre, move out to the left side, work three movements, back to the centre and out to the right side, work three movements. Finish the movement again in the centre of the forehead (movement **139**).

2. Now, turn the hands, fingers together, facing towards the nose and smooth out across the forehead to the temples. With the middle finger of both hands, press into the temple, hold the pressure to the count of

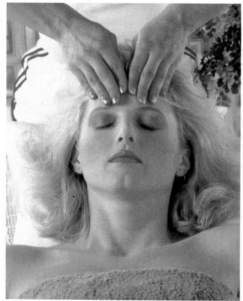

140

141

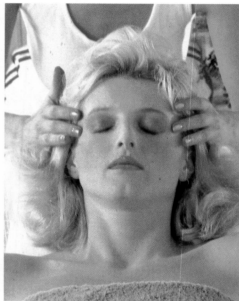

142

143

144

three and then release the pressure and return to the centre of the forehead.

With the hands in the same position, pull up the forehead from the eyebrows towards the hairline. Work first to the left side of the forehead, then to the right and finish back at the centre. Repeat the movement three times and finish at the centre of the forehead (movements **140**, **141** and **142**).

3. Now, interlock your fingers so that the middle finger of your right hand is placed between the first and middle fingers of your left hand and circle across the forehead from left to right, finishing in the centre. Turn your hands, fingers together, facing the nose and smooth out to the temples and hold the pressure, then release (movements **143** and **144**).

145

146

4. With the ring finger of both hands, work small circles from the outer corners of the eyes in towards the nose; turn the hands and bring the fingers lightly up the side of the nose and apply a slight pressure at the junction of the nose and eyebrow. Repeat three times, finishing finally at the centre of the forehead and smooth out to the temple as before (movements **145** and **146**).

5. Bring your hands down to the left hand side of the face and with the two middle fingers of each hand slowly work over the jawline from outer mouth to ear. Repeat three times. Lift the muscles and feel them respond to your pressure (movements **147** and **148**).

147

148

6. Continue up the side of the face in a line from the side of the nose out towards the middle of the ear. Finish off the movement by the left temple, move the right hand across to the right temple then apply pressure and release (movements **149** and **150**).

7. Now, commence the same movement on the right side, finishing off at the right temple, bringing the left hand across the forehead to the left temple and applying pressure as before.

8. Place your thumbs on top of the

150

chin and circle over the chin to the count of three. Now, work around the mouth with both thumbs until you reach the centre of the top lip. Break off the movement and return to the chin and repeat smoothing the mouth and easing out the strain. Finish off at the centre of the top lip and bring hands down to underneath the chin and then circle out along the jawline towards the ears. This area gets very tense and a slow pressure helps to ease the strain. Repeat three times (movements **151**, **152**, **153**, **154** and **155**).

151

152

153

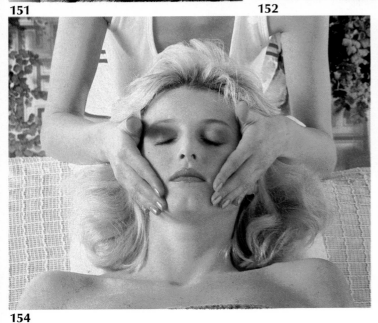

154

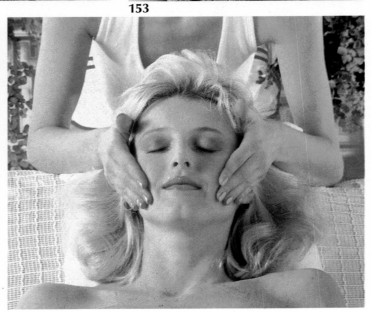

155

156

157

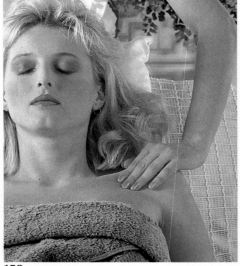

158

159

160

161

162

9. Finish off below the ears and then massage the neck with broad, round strokes. At the base of the neck, drop your hands over the chest and make large circles ending at the back of the neck. You should end this stroke at the back of the neck, into the base of the skull. Now, bring your hands back to the jawline by the ears and begin to tap lightly along the jawline starting at the left hand side and working along to the right hand side and back again. The movement should be a light tapping with the finger tips, first the left hand, then the right hand, in a 1, 2; 1, 2 tempo. This is a good movement for a flabby jawline. End the movement under the chin (movements **156**, **157**, **158**, **159**, **160**, **161** and **162**).

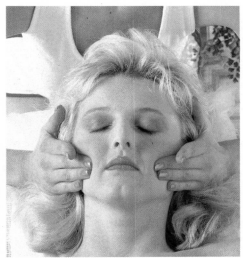

164

10. Now, slide your fingers out to the ears and then up the cheekbone by the hairline and gently lift the cheekbones with the two middle fingers of each hand. Move in towards the nose. Repeat three times and end by the nose (movements **163** and **164**).

11. Slide up the nose and with both thumbs on the opposite sides of the nose, circle the sides of the nose and then bring your thumbs to the top of the nose and circle up the nose to the top of the forehead. Your thumbs, when you change from the side of the nose to the top, will be in the

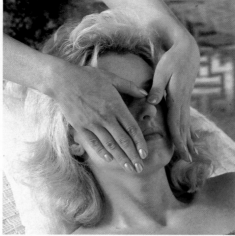

165

166

167

correct position to circle up the nose and over the forehead. At the top of the forehead, slide the thumbs out to the temple and press and release temple pressure as before (movements **165**, **166** and **167**).

12. Move your hands, with your fingers extended and your thumbs to the back of the head, over the hair and slowly circle the head with increasing pressure (movement **168**).

Finish off the massage with forehead stroking movements in exactly the same way as you commenced the facial and gently ease off at the third stroke.

Facial massage is extremely helpful to the over-tense and nervous individual and is a good way to begin a full body massage. It eases headaches, releases tension and can help drain sinuses and relieve puffy eyes. If you do not have time to give a full massage, the facial massage will be just the thing to relax and refresh your partner.

Herbalists

Baldwins, Walworth Road, Elephant and Castle, London.

Aromatic Oil Company, 12 Littlegate Street, Oxford.

168